The Further Adventures of
Bix Beiderbecke

JAZZ BAND CLASSICS FOR TRUMPET

T0081478

To access audio visit:
www.halleonard.com/mylibrary

Enter Code
4783-4478-0295-7139

ISBN 978-1-59615-741-5

Music Minus One

EXCLUSIVELY DISTRIBUTED BY

HAL•LEONARD®

Visit Hal Leonard Online at
www.halleonard.com

Contact Us:
Hal Leonard
7777 West Bluemound Road
Milwaukee, WI 53213
Email: info@halleonard.com

In Europe contact:
Hal Leonard Europe Limited
42 Wigmore Street
Marylebone, London, W1U 2RN
Email: info@halleonardeurope.com

In Australia contact:
Hal Leonard Australia Pty. Ltd.
4 Lentara Court
Cheltenham, Victoria, 3192 Australia
Email: info@halleonard.com.au

BIX: SHORT TIME

by Richard M. Sudhalter

Leon Beiderbecke wasn't around for long. He dominated the jazz world for far less than a decade, hitting his real artistic peak for two years, in 1927 and '28. The rest of the time he spent learning his craft—or, latterly, trying to recover from the alcoholism that finally killed him.

Yet Bix, as he was known, quickly emerged as the major stylistic force in the new music, equivalent to Louis Armstrong among blacks. His way of playing the cornet, his way of treating material, became a beloved standard for white musicians.

When he died, both too soon and as a wreck of the healthy young man he'd been, the news devastated the ranks of musicians who had accepted his gospel as the most civilized and effective way to play jazz, "It was," said one saxophonist, "as if the Pope had died. We couldn't imagine what to do next."

Therein lies the mystery of his life, death and entire existence. How did a musician so briefly there, so much an insider to the musical community, last so long as an influence? Why do players many years after his demise still listen to his approximately 250 records, period pieces all, and willingly take their influence to heart?

In so ephemeral a music as jazz it's a wonder for his image to have had such longevity and to have held such power. But how, and why? No other single musician can have that claim made for him—even Jack Teagarden and PeeWee Russell, standing individuals both, did not spread their influence through the entire music world as did Bix Beiderbecke.

Yet today, so many years after his passing, there is still a "Bix way" of phrasing, or construction, even of emotional temperature, which tracks back to him with the accuracy of a woodsman's trail. That in itself furnishes a clue to the lasting appeal of Bix Beiderbecke.

In its early days jazz was not a complex music. Its chief soloists—led by Armstrong and Bechet —had styles that were commanding and demanding, and emotionally simple. Louis playing "Potato Head Blues," for example, was a messenger from a higher power. Straightforward, direct, simple. It said what it had to say, no more or less.

By comparison a solo by Bix, regardless of tempo or character, seems complex to an unlikely degree. In his most abandoned moments there is just a hint of sadness, or at least contemplation. His thoughtful solos are likewise loaded with contradictions. As a noted critic and Bix admirer once put it, Arnstrong demands your attention; Bix invites you in and entreats the ear to pay attention.

⁂

He was born in the up-and-coming Mississippi riverside community of Davenport, Iowa, on the 10th of March, 1903. His was a family tied by social obligation to its community. His father, named Bismark in obvious deference to Germany's "iron chancellor," was a staid traditionalist, determined that his second son not waste a lifetime's opportunities on anything so insubstantial as professional dance music, which for him was *Gebrauchsmusik,* just a small cut above trash collection.

For Beiderbecke *père,* music was something you made for fun and according to strict social rules—in a marching band or singing in a *Mannerchor*. It was hardly a view shared by his wife, Agatha, or by his other children. As he saw it, if the boy showed signs of wanting to play in dance orchestras, the time had long since arrived for him to join his father selling lumber for a living to contractors and other sorts of merchants.

It quickly became clear that "Bickie," as he was called by friends and family, had an ear for music of a rather less disciplined sort than was to Bismark's liking. And when he set out to teach himself to play a friend's cornet, the father's reaction was something less than favorable.

Charles, his elder brother, returned from military training at the end of the first World War with a gift: several new phonograph records and a wind-up machine to play them on. They were quickly adopted by young Bix, who especially favored selections by the Original Dixieland Jazz Band.

Family and friends recalled the lad playing them, slowing them down to learn the notes and emerging as a promising young performer on the instrument.

There is no doubt that he worked hard at it and that the work yielded results. By the time he was 20, he was a *de facto* leader of a band of youthful musicians who called themselves the Wolverine Orchestra, playing at a roadhouse called the Stockton Club near Hamilton, Ohio, about 20 miles south of Cincinnati.

Nobody knew it, but this formed a clear beginning to Bix's professional career. The Wolverines, with Bix's horn leading, developed a new concept of ensemble play and rhythm. It converted any ensemble lead into a flowing melodic line.

The band was far from perfect, with tenor saxophonist George Johnson and trombonist Al Gandee particularly guilty of wrong notes and aimless ensemble lines. Drummer Vic Moore often rushed his breaks. Others were equally guilty of infractions great and small.

But Bix's lead horn, and Bobby Gillette's banjo lift produced a kind of four-to-the-bar rhythm that was smoother than the jerky syncopations of the Original Dixieland Jazz band and crisper then the New Orleans lilt of the Rhythm Kings. Colleagues hearing it for the first time spoke of hearing "sock-time," in which each instrument in its way emphasized each of the four beats of every bar.

It all congealed in February of 1924 when the Wolverines, after a characteristically depressing night at Doyle's, a particularly uninspiring Cincinnati Dancing School, drove 125 miles to Richmond, Indiana, to make two records for the Gennett division of the Starr Piano Company.

The company had already recorded King Oliver's Creole Jazz Band, the New Orleans Rhythm Kings and Indiana's Hitch's Happy Harmonists in their quest for new talent. Only two titles were deemed fit for issue, but "Fidgety Feet" and "The Jazz Me Blues" introduced a new cornet talent and approach to listeners.

Two qualities—"correlated" phrasing and a reliance on the cornet's vocal middle register—seemed to characterize Bix's stylistic approach. Their records, made over the year that followed, found them all playing more confidently and with more skill. In May they recorded "Riverboat Shuffle," first work by Indiana

pianist Hoagy Carmichael, and June 20th found them attacking "I Need Some Pettin'," with Vic Berton doing the more skilled drumming.

It was perhaps inevitable that Bix's cornet work with the Wolverines would draw big-time attention, and toward year's end Detroit's premiere bandleader Jean Goldkette came to call. No surprise, then, that Monday, November 24, found Bix among Fuzzy Farrar, Bill Rank and Goldkette's other featured men making records for the Victor Company at the Detroit Athletic Club.

They loved Bix's playing, and gave the newcomer an extended solo on one title, only to have recording supervisor Eddie King veto it for issue. "He just didn't like that kind of jazz from the very first hearing," pianist Paul Mertz recalled. "He then changed the spot over to [lead trumpet Fuzzy] Farrar for the Henry Busse type of polite trumpet he preferred."

But there was no stopping him, and within a few months Bix was in St. Louis, appearing in an orchestra led by Frank Trumbauer, the famed C-melody sax virtuoso, and including clarinet and sax individualist Charles "PeeWee" Russell. We can but guess how good this band was, because they didn't record. But Beiderbecke emerged from this experience a seasoned musician, who was welcomed to the Goldkette Victor Recording Orchestra soon after.

The Goldkette Orchestra came east for the first time in the autumn of 1926. met and vanquished the Fletcher Henderson band in a battle of music at Roseland Ballroom."We were supposed to be the kings, the greatest thing in New York," said cornetist Rex Stewart. "Then, suddenly, up pops this band of Johnny-come-latelies from out in the sticks...and they just *creamed* us.

"You know, I worshipped Louis [Armstrong] at that time, tried to walk like him, talk like him, even dress like him. He was God to me, and to all the other cats, too. Then, all of a sudden comes this white boy from out west, playin' stuff all his own. Didn't sound like Louis or anybody else. But just so pretty. And that *tone* he got. Knocked us all out."

He continued to knock them out on records, and when the Goldkette Orchestra collapsed and he joined the brass section of the mighty "King of Jazz," Paul Whiteman, in 1927. Suddenly there were Bix collectors, mostly fans, for whom one bar of Beiderbecke was enough to make a Whiteman record a valuable commodity. News about him and his exploits spread quickly through what more than one colleague called the "musician underground."

He appeared in band pictures, including advertisements for band instruments. Was the only Whiteman sideman singled out—although he played no solo—in a newsreel commemorating the band's move from Victor to the Columbia label. His appearance on a record was enough to guarantee sales.

But with all the attention came increased reliance on alcohol. Bix had always drunk his share, but there came a time when the habit became an addiction. No one would say anything or be more specific, but it was clear that shortly after joining Whiteman the young man with a horn had become an addicted young man, who seemed able to play only when he was drunk.

Yet Bix's charm continued. Just to see him, smiling broadly, in Whiteman's Orchestra seemed enough to cure all ills. But it was not so. In September of 1928, during a record session, the unthinkable happened Emotionally and physically worn down, Bix found it impossible to go on. He spent time in a hospital for addiction, returned to Davenport for a "cure," swore he was off liquor for good.

All to no avail. In the end, after returning to New York for one final try—even moving out to Queens to get away from the scores of fellow-musicians who followed him everywhere, Bix contracted pneumonia and on a hot night in August, 1931, died during a seizure of delirium tremens.

But he left behind one nagging question, which refuses to vanish: why does a fresh-faced young man, whose stay in the music business was less than a decade, leave behind a legacy so rich and varied? It has little to do with the cornet, in that styles and personalities have changed over the years, and even the disciples—Jimmy McPartland, Andy Secrest, Stirling Bose and others—are gone.

Not the piano or the pieces that appeared under his name. Or the records, most of which belong to their times. No—it has more to do with the idea that no musical message is simple. That complexity exists in every utterance we make. If Armstrong indulged in simple statements, Bix's were indirect, complex. No solo, even the most jubilant, was free of an underlying sadness; even the saddest solo—*I'm Comin' Virginia,* for example—is lifted by a hint of a happy ending,

The idea of restraint in a jazz solo found its two great champions in Bix and in his musical friend, Frank Trumbauer. When the pair performed together they set one another off, serious and light. Bardic and jolly. Bix able to play straight man to Tram's levity In all, there was nothing in jazz to equal them. Armstrong, then at the top of the heap in music, recognized and praised Bix's high seriousness. Still, so many years after his departure, we listen to him and marvel.

Is it his tone, crisp and clean as a summer morning? His restraint, so different from other jazzmen of his times? The complexity written in to his every solo? Or does it have to do with the sweetness of his playing. so appealing to us all? Or are we talking of some combination. some blending of qualities which makes him special?

Or do we reverence the very idea of the promising artist, dead long before his time? People who have never read a poem revere the memory of Wilfred Owen, a needless casualty of the first World War. In James Joyce, our hearts thrill to the very idea of young, ill Michael Furey singing love songs in the rain outside Gretta's nighttime window.

What quality about them do we cherish? What is it about Bix Beiderbecke that even those not captivated by his music will dub him Jazz's number one saint? Perhaps the very brevity of his stay among us, so talented yet so blighted by addiction, tells an eloquent tale. Would to Bix story have been the same if he had lived and his talent had aged with him?

We don't—will never—know. We need only be thankful for his brief, semi-obscure presence among us. For the fact that once, in a galaxy far away, he sang his emotional little song for us, and that song rings and shines for us still to this day.

I'M COMING VIRGINIA

Often played in E♭ (concert key), with the verse in E♭m. Sometimes it is played in F. Bix's famous solo is in F so we give you both keys.

Heywood / Cook 1925
Transc./ Arr. Peter Ecklund

CHINA BOY

An old pop tune that became a traditional jazz favorite. The original melody is quite square, so syncopation and repeated notes must be added, as they are here. The Bix solo is from a Paul Whiteman recording.

Winfree / Boutalje 1922
Transc./Arr. Peter Ecklund

10

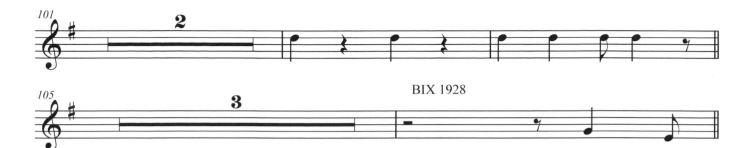

BIX 1928

ENS. LEAD

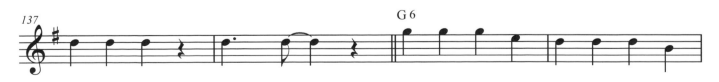

JAZZ ME BLUES

This arrangement comes from two of the not very many recordings that feature Bix throughout with a standard traditional jazz front line of cornet, clarinet, and trombone. The 1924 solo was originally in F concert. Today the tune is almost always played in E♭.

Tom Delaney 1921
Transc./Arr. Peter Ecklund

19

C7   BIX 1927

D7   G7

C7   F   F/A

D7   G7

F   F   A7   A7   Dm   Dm   D7   D7/F♯

G7   C7   F   B♭6   F   F7   E7   E♭7

D7   G7

C7   F   F/A

D7   G7

F   F   A7   A7   Dm   Dm   D7

G7   C7   F   B♭6   F   C7   F   C13 F

RIVERBOAT SHUFFLE

This tune is usually played in E♭ concert (with the verse in Gm) although Bix never recorded it in that key. Notice that the chords of the chorus are almost the same as for "I Can't Give You Anything But Love" and "Pennies From Heaven."

Hoagy Carmichael 1924
Transc./Arr. Peter Ecklund

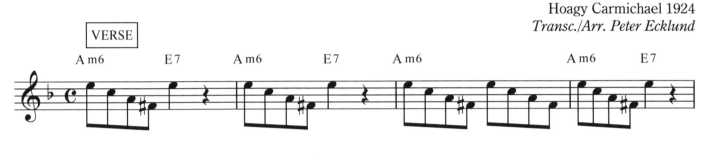

BIX 1924

BIX 1927

BLUE BIX

An original tune based on a chromatic
ascending phrase that Bix liked to play.

Peter Ecklund

WAY DOWN YONDER IN NEW ORLEANS

This tune has an unusual number of bars (24) and uses nothing but tonic and dominant chords for the first 14. The Jazz Police have found a violation in bar 10. The chord should be Am7 or G, but D7 is often used.

Creamer/ Layton 1922
Transc./Arr. Peter Ecklund

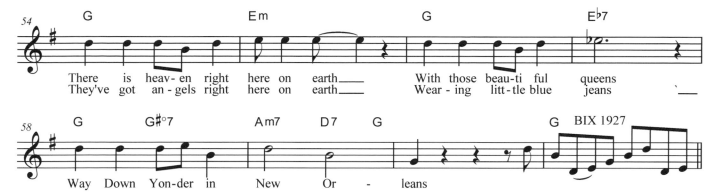

There is heav-en right here on earth___ With those beau-ti ful queens
They've got an-gels right here on earth___ Wear-ing litt-tle blue jeans

Way Down Yon-der in New Or - leans

BIX 1927

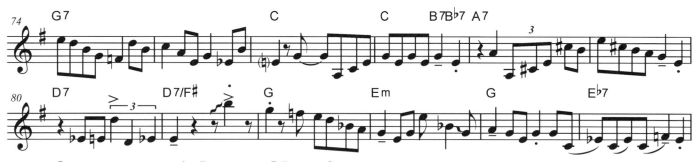

ENS. LEAD

BABY WON'T YOU PLEASE COME HOME

Don't study the original too closely here. Some notes in Bix's playful solo
had to be changed to fit the harmonies of the song as it is played today.

Warfields / Williams 1919
Transc./Arr. Peter Ecklund

SWEET SUE

One of a handful of tunes from the trad repetoire that are usually played in G concert. This recording by the Potted Palm Orchestra features some exotic mutes. The Solotone or Mega-Mute looks like a straight mute inserted into another straight mute. It may cause the horn to go sharp and require a tuning adjustment. The Derby mute looks like a hat made of aluminum or fiberglass. Both mutes are still available.

by Will Harris & Victor Young 1928
Transc./Arr. Peter Ecklund

26

ROYAL GARDEN BLUES

The ensemble lead and the second solo are from the 1927 Bix and his Gang recording. The first Bix solo comes from the 1924 Wolverines session. Notice the 1920's dance tempo. This tune is often played too fast today.

S. Williams / C. Williams 1919
Transc./Arr. Peter Ecklund

SINGIN' THE BLUES

Conrad / Robinson / Lewis / Young 1920
Transc./Arr. Peter Ecklund

MMO 3853

(FRANK TRUMBAUR'S SAX SOLO 1927)

BIX 1927

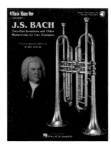

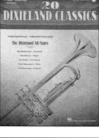